Breaking the Chains: From Hurting to Healing

By:

Dr. Catrina Pullum

Published by:

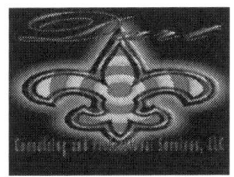

Dart Consulting and Professional Services, LLC.

Dart Consulting and Professional Services, LLC.
P.O. Box 56554
New Orleans, La. 70156-6554
www.dartconsultingllc.org
(504) 452-0110

Design & Photos: PullCorp Media Group/PRW

Editor: PullCorp Media Group

Copyright © 2014 Dr. Catrina Pullum All rights reserved.

No part of this book may be reproduced by any mechanical, photographic, or electronic process, or in the form of a phonographic recording; nor may it be stored in a retrieval system, transmitted, nor be copied for public or private use. Unless otherwise stated, all scripture quotations are taken from the Holy Bible, King James Version.

Library of Congress Cataloging-in-Publication Data

2014909162

ISBN: 978-0-9899215-1-0 (sc)
978-0-9899215-2-7 (e)

Table of Contents

The Dedication

Foreword

Acknowledgements

Introduction

Chain Reaction

The Cycle Perpetuates

Buffering the Pain

My Pain is my Purpose

Plan of the Enemy

The Master's Plan

The Chains are Broken

The Dedication

The world at times can be a cold, mean and evil place. Though it is filled with great people it also has its share of predators. No matter what, we all sin and fall short of the glory of God and need a Savior, one that has come to save us all.

In Breaking the Chains: From Hurting to Healing, I take you the reader on a journey through my life (which I am sure is not only my story), which is a true from trials to triumph story. Throughout my life, I have experienced horrific incidents from being sexually abused at church, living in a domestic violence relationship, being born to a teen mother and later becoming one, alcoholism, divorce and more.

In spite of my life's circumstances, today I am Dr. Pullum, because I have always maintained a relationship with God. My faith in and relationship with God has allowed me to survive, maintain my sanity and somehow move pass the pain. I know today that the pain was all a part of my purpose. I use my story to help as many people as I can to fight through the pain and free themselves from the chains that can hold a person that has survived sexual, physical and mental assaults and all other forms of abuse hostage. Many aspects of my story I still have never revealed for an assortment of reasons however now it is finally time to do so. I promise to tell the truth, the whole truth and nothing but the truth because it is my story but it is all for God's glory. I am free, no more chains holding me and I have dedicated my story to everyone that has survived something; together we are FREE!!

My story is dedicated to you….

To the woman that has endured years of domestic abuse in the name of love, for the girl being touched inappropriately that has no one to share her hurt with, for the boy who's struggling with his sexual identity because he would been abused so long by a man in his life that he cannot identify who he is today, for the mother who's been mentally abused so long that her self-esteem is no longer existent. If no one hears you, I do. I hear you and I understand. I am now using my voice to give you your voice back!! YOU HAVE THE RIGHT TO NO LONGER BE SILENT, TO SPEAK OUT AND TO LIVE!!

Foreword:

"On a fall afternoon, I walked across the hall from my bedroom to the bathroom. There, I rifled through our mirrored medicine cabinet, bypassing typical over-the-counter items in favor of the first bottle of painkillers I found. With my fingers wrapped around the slim cylinder, I returned to my room and closed the door. As the sun gilded the edges of my window curtains, I emptied the whole bottle of pills into my hand. I stared at them for a long time before chasing them down with water. Then I sank into bed and closed my eyes.

As I waited to die, I wasn't thinking about losing my father or my faith. I wasn't thinking about my mother, her heavy hands and long absences, which often left me in charge of my four younger siblings. I wasn't thinking of the many people who had inappropriately touched me, and my thoughts did not land on my boyfriend, who was too busy pursuing other girls to notice the pain in my eyes. I never thought about the person who would find me lying in bed with an empty bottle of pills on the floor. I wasn't even thinking of my unborn baby, though my belly was stretched far and thin with her eight-month growth. All I could think about was escaping my pain. I was fifteen."

If you think that story was heartbreaking and unique – think again. Dr. Catrina Pullum, in "Breaking the Chains" shares a story with many similarities to mine.

Unfortunately, millions of other people share our tragic experiences. From being raised by her grandmothers, to being abused by people she trusted - Dr. Pullum's story will take you on a journey experienced by countless others. All too often, parents sit around wondering "what the hell happened to my kid? How did my precious, precious child become this unrecognizable person? Why are they smoking, drinking, doing drugs, having multiple sex partners and babies before they are grown?"

Far too many adults have become obsessed with bigger houses, more luxurious automobiles, the latest mobile phones or pointless customized services, often at the expense of our young people. We have missed signs that horrible, unspeakable, downright unimaginable things have happened to them. We provide essential things for them, but oftentimes we are chasing an evaporating dream. Perhaps that's one of the reasons why we miss critical, life changing moments. Perhaps its why some children have been doing drugs for years, or why a young girl is six months pregnant before anyone notices. Supposedly our children are our future. Allegedly they're a gift from God and too precious to lose. But sometimes, we treat them as dispensable rags. Conversely as parents, caregivers, educators, relatives, friends, and even strangers, it is *our* responsibility to help them grow into happy, healthy, productive adults. We must properly invest in them. That's our only hope for better world and a better tomorrow.

Trouble has found Dr. Pullum and me, on many occasions. Life has presented us with extraordinary challenges. It's because of those challenges we have a special place in our hearts for people who are hurting. It doesn't matter if it's from abuse, rejection, loss of a loved one, sickness, or something that makes them feel worthless, we know and we understand. I'm grateful she requested I write the foreword to her book. It's people like us, who can help change the future for our children. If you know someone who cannot see through their pain, please give them a copy of this book. Its proof Dr. Pullum and you care - *together you can help change their world.*

To Dr. Pullum, I say *thank you*! Thank you for having the courage to share your story with the world. We are going to help save the next generation of young people from a world of destruction.

Toni L. Coleman Carter, Chief Inspirational Strategist

Author of *When Trouble Finds You*

www.wtfu2.org

Acknowledgements:

I must first thank the almighty, omniscient, ever present God who is the head of my life. Without him I would be nothing, but it's because of him that I am all that I am today. He's never left nor forsaken me but has always been there for me. All of my days I owe him praise.

With humble gratitude and love, I must acknowledge the following people for allowing me to share my story and supporting my vision.

To my right & left hand, partner in business and in life my husband, Shawn. I am so Blessed to have you in my life. When we met, my life began. Thank you for allowing me to be me and being so supportive of the vision that God has given me. Love you so much! More than you will ever know.

To my children and family, who supported and encouraged me in spite of all the time it took me away from them. It was a long and difficult journey for them. D'Mari, Ruby, Sharae, & Christian, I am thankful to God that he has allowed me to be your mom. You all are very intelligent and gifted. Thank you to my mom (Glenda) and stepfather (Rogers) for allowing me to live with your grandmother (Mary) at her request. I was special to have three mothers in my life. Thank you for being there for me and encouraging me to follow my dreams.

WOW! Thank you to my grandmother (Alderaine) who was just happy with me having a high school diploma after I got pregnant. I am proud to say that I superseded her expectations. Thank you for partaking in raising me and teaching me how to be lady. Thank you for loving me in spite of you not knowing some of the things that I did was a result of being hurt. Thank you to my uncles (Eddie Sr., Robert Jr., Darryl, Ronald Sr., & Owen, Sr.) for emulating fatherhood so well, that I can call you dad or I could ask you to do fatherly things for me. Thank you for protecting me even today. Thank you so much for being there any time that I need you. Thank you for being unselfish and allowing me to serve others. I love you all.

 To my PullCorp Media & Center of Empowerment Family, thank you all for being patient for allowing me to birth the vision that God has given me. Thank you to my spiritual sister & friend, Annette of Dart Consulting & Professional Service, for bringing my vision to pass and for your support. Thank you to my sister from another mother, A Conrad, who has always been there with a listening ear and supported my vision from the day we met. Thank you to Taylor for stepping in when I was unavailable. Thank you to Mr. Carter, our Branding Manager, for designing my book cover and all of graphics for my book. Thank you and your fiancé, Phylea for working with me around the clock to make this project a success. Thank you to the whole PullCorp Media & COE Family for your support. Thank you to my Puissance Maison Productions Family for producing my book signing.

    Thank you to my sister, Toni Carter, for completing my foreword for me. Thank you for allowing me to share my story with you and for your feedback. May God continue to bless you!

To my guardian angels, great grandmother (Mary) and my grandfather (Melvin) I miss you all so much. Grandmother, thank you for raising me to be a God Fearing young woman. Thank you for teaching me that God is my GPS. Thank you for teaching me to serve and empower others. Thank you for setting the standard for me. Thank you to my grandfather for accepting me as his own and raising me and my older son. Thank you for spoiling us at the same time teaching us a value of a dollar. I know you and grandmother are smiling down on me and my family.

Restraint

When referencing the word **re·straint** [ri stráynt] in the dictionary, it defines the word as meaning:

1. holding back: an act or the quality of holding back, limiting, or controlling something
2. restraining thing: something that controls or limits somebody or something
3. holding device: something that is fastened to limit somebody's freedom of movement

In many instances when we think of something being restrained, we may visualize the restraining mechanism as handcuffs or a chain. We associate handcuffs being used to restrain someone involved in criminal activities and chains being utilized to restrain any and everything else from slaves to bicycles. I've not been on the wrong side of the law therefore I cannot attest to the restraining power of handcuffs, and though I've never been physically bound, I can still tell you what it's like to have chains on your life. Chains that bind you. The chains that prohibit one from escaping the grips of their past, the chains that bind and won't allow for easy transition into the destiny God has ordained. The chains that cannot be seen, but are very real. Chains………

Binding Chains

Chains are a series of connected links which are typically made of metal and may consist of two or more links. Chains are usually made in one of two styles, according to their intended use:

- a. Those designed for lifting, such as when used with a hoist for pulling; or for securing, such as with a bicycle lock,
- b. Those designed for transferring power in machines have links designed to mesh with the teeth of the sprockets of the machine, and are flexible in only one dimension. They are called roller chains.

Chains are durable and strong and are capable of lifting, securing and holding whatever it is attached to in place, allowing minimal to no movement, growth or ability to be free. Therefore, what it holds can be considered as stagnant. Just as chains have been used to restrain objects they have also been used in some instances to restrain people both physically and mentally.

Just as one may use a chain to restrain his or her bicycle so that no one else can take it, slave owners used chains back in the days of slavery, to kept slaves confined. Confining slaves limited their flexibility so that they would not run away or escape and kept them stagnant, which killed their desire to thrive, ability to dream and succeed. Their movement was limited, therefore, they were limited. The chains did not allow them to escape their current enslaved situation and reach a place of freedom. It caused them to remain in a place most unpleasant, to become complacent with a life of hopelessness, no hope for a better life. Their past was also their present and was destined to be their future. The chains were just that powerful, they were a hindrance.

In Breaking The Chains: From Hurting to Healing, I'll be speaking against the chains that are not visible to the human eye. Chains that bind, but cannot be touched. Chains that restrain, but cannot be easily revealed. Mental chains that physically cripple us. Chains on our minds that hinder our ability to move, limit our ability to live free, hinder our transition into purpose. Chains of a horrific past (drug abuse, sexual abuse, neglect, etc.) that hinder our progression into the future God has in store for us.

Invisible chains that bind…..
Chains on our minds………
Chains on our lives……….

God did not design us to be shackled or restrained but to be free. In John 8:36 it tells us whom the son has set free, is free indeed. Jesus purpose for taking on the physical form of man was so that we would be free. He died so that we would live free and he rose again so we would be free from sin, sickness and all that would bind us from moving freely into our purpose and living a life ordained by God.

Living free is Ordained

Galatians 5:13 says, "You, my brothers, were called to be free. But do not use your freedom to indulge the sinful nature; rather, serve one another in love."

Galatians 5:1 says, "It is for freedom that Christ has set us free. Stand firm, then, and do not let yourselves be burdened again by a yoke of slavery."

Colossians 1:13-14 For he has rescued us from the dominion of darkness and brought us into the Kingdom of the Son he loves, in whom we have redemption, the forgiveness of sins.

Chain Reaction

Job 36: 8-9

But if people are bound in chains, held fast by cords of affliction, he tells them what they have done—
that they have sinned arrogantly.

The Patterns of Our Lives

There are patterns established in most families what we commonly refer to as traditions. Sometimes, family traditions are associated with practices and beliefs which are handed over from one generation to the next generation. The flow of family traditions proceeds effortlessly from one generation to the next extending from immediate family and later including extended families (e.g. individuals that marry into the family). These traditions ensure that the bond of unity within the family are established and continues to grow. In the modern context, maintaining and developing family traditions continue to be as significant as it was in at the earliest times.

Some great family traditions are monthly game/movie nights, traditional birthday meals, specific days to put up Christmas trees, specific holiday meal times and much more. As for our family, our family's tradition is that on Sundays we attend church together, come home, and eat as a family. Also for holidays, we as an entire family have to go to my grandmother's house and celebrate the holiday with over eating and enjoying family.

There have been other patterns that repeated within my family which are not necessarily positive or what we would label as traditions, however, they've been consistent. We wouldn't label them as traditions because these behaviors are not encouraged to be repeated, unfortunately they are. They're more of the family's vicious cycles. Vicious family cycles are those such as cycles of poverty, teen pregnancy, engagement in at-risk behaviors, etc.

The cycle of poverty is the set of factors or events by which poverty is initially established and will continue unless there's some external intervention (e.g. one member attains education from an institute of higher learning) breaking the cycle.

Such families have either limited or no resources causing them to face many difficulties that make it almost impossible to break the cycle. Poverty-stricken families tend to lack the opportunity or the know how to access the things that will deliver them from their present state of poverty (education, entrepreneurship options, access to capital, etc.). This lack of knowledge allows the cycle to perpetuate and they remain poor throughout their lives. Poor parents pass these behaviors on to their kids, which in turn are passed on to their kids and the cycle continues and cannot easily be changed. Not impossible but not at all easy.

Chain Reaction

A **chain reaction** is a sequence of reactions where a reactive product or by-product causes additional reactions to take place. In a chain reaction, positive feedback leads to a self-amplifying chain of events.

The dictionary gives three meanings to the phrase "chain reaction" for physics, chemistry and the other generally speaking. In Physics, it's a self-sustaining reaction in which the fission of nuclei of one generation of nuclei produces particles that cause the fission of at least an equal number of nuclei of the succeeding generation. In Chemistry, it's defined as a reaction that results in a product necessary for the continuance of the reaction. In general it's defined as a series of events in which each event is the result of the event preceding and the cause of the event following.

The Bible also discusses chain reactions though it does not use the term. Let me tell you about a spiritual chain reaction that has the power to transform our lives. It begins in Psalm 119:69: "Let my cry come before You, O Lord; give me understanding according to Your word." Prayer leads to understanding. This is the first part of the chain reaction. Do you pray for understanding as you read your Bible? Do you pray, "Open my eyes, that I may see wondrous things from Your law" (Psalm 119:18)?

Next, understanding leads to freedom. "Let my supplication come before You; deliver me according to your word" (v. 170). The psalmist asks for the freedom that comes from the truth of God. Jesus said, "You shall know the truth, and the truth shall make you free" ([John 8:32](#)). The greatest bondage in the world is the bondage to lies. If you believe a lie, you are in slavery; but if you believe God's truth, you live in freedom.

The third stage in this spiritual chain reaction is found in verse 171: "My lips shall utter praise, for you teach me Your statutes." Freedom leads to praise. When we understand the statutes of God, we can sing. Knowing His Word makes us want to praise Him.

Finally, praise leads to witnessing. "My tongue shall speak of your word, for all

Your commandments are righteousness" (v. 172). As a result of our witness, people may come to know Jesus Christ as their Savior.

For the purpose of this book we will delve into the general meaning of "chain reaction". In a nutshell it's almost like a snowball effect, in which a small snowball eventually causes a larger snowball until finally you have an avalanche.

My chain reaction occurrence was that of becoming a teen mother and how this cycle repeated itself in my life. The other components of the cycle did not hold truth for me simply because I had access to resources that not only afforded me many opportunities and which allowed me the ability to escape the cycle. I was the outlander.

The Cycle Perpetuates

Isaiah 40:8

The grass withers, the flower fades but the Word of God will stand forever.

The Cycle Continues

We should all know what a cycle looks like. It appears as a sequence of repeated events. The sun rising and setting is a cycle. As women, we encounter a less enjoyable cycle in our lives on a monthly basis until we become of age. This cycle is a lot less pleasurable than that of the sun rising and setting however it's a part of life.

There are also cycles in life which may be encountered by individuals and families. Family cycles including going from childhood, to being a teen, getting married, parenting and elderly stages. We also have negative connotations regarding cycles such as vicious family cycles. Vicious family cycles include poverty, drug abuse and teen-pregnancy to name a few.

My great-grandmother aspired to intercede and break what had happened in our family in the hope of preventing what was becoming a cycle. Though my mom had me as a teen mother, it was the hopes of my great grandmother that if she had raise me, I would not encounter the same fate. It was not due to a lack of effort on the part of my great-grandmother or my grandmother, but due to my poor decision making that I fell into the cycle and allowed it to repeat itself.

It was never my intention to repeat the mistakes of my mother or to disappoint my grandparents; I was just doing what all the teens were doing. I allowed myself to fall victim to peer pressure because all of my friends were having sex. So, I had met a guy and decided it must be the thing to do. Being immature, not thinking past the moment, not thinking if I do this that I would quite possibly have a baby, I did not stop to think of the potential consequences to my actions and that I would be doing the same thing my mom did, becoming a mother before the time that I was prepared to do so. It was supposed to be a carefree time in life, yet because of one decision, to engage in a grown-up activity, one time, my whole path changed. My life was no longer carefree, but careful because now every decision I made no longer impacted only me but would impact the life of myself and my child. My life had taken a shift, and the shift for me felt like a punishment. Although I now understand that at times God places us in uncomfortable situations to make us better, that was not my level of understanding as a child.

Shifting the Cycle

Charles Darwin once stated, "It is not the strongest of the species that survives, nor the most intelligent, but rather the one most responsive to change." Change is inevitable and has always been a necessary aspect of life and work. Our world is changing more rapidly than ever. No matter how much we want to believe we are not changing, due to the fact that the world is ever evolving, this means we are experiencing constant change. If you do not believe me, try running like you did ten (10) years ago, not going to happen ☺.

It is likely that you will have to cope with a variety of changes in the course and scope of your life. Changes in your career due to lack of fulfillment, layoffs or retirement; changes in family due to marriage, divorce or death; physical changes in well-being due to illness, weight loss/gain, etc. However, the issue is not change itself as much as it is the manner in which you adapt to change. Change is not something that can be abruptly done. In fact, change has five (5) stages: pre-contemplation, contemplation, preparation, action, and maintenance.

Pre-contemplation is the stage where you are either not aware of a problem or are aware of an issue but have no intention to change the situation.

Contemplation is where the person comes to the realization that there is a problem and they think of steps to resolve or overcome it.

Preparation is when action will be taken in the next month to resolve the problem.

Action is the stage in which individuals modify their behavior, experiences, or environment in order to overcome their problems. Action involves the most overt behavioral changes and requires considerable commitment of time and energy.

Maintenance: After the behavior has been changed, people must consistently apply what is learned in the action stage to avoid returning back to or reliving the problem.

As a teenager I can admit that I knew nothing about the cycle of change nor the steps that are listed above. What I did know was that I would encounter several changes in my life, some rather unpleasant and I did not want to continue in this cycle. Something deep within me told me there would be many more changes that I would have to encounter in life and it was up to me and God to assure they were different and even better on some level. I knew that, even though I loved my mother I did not want my life to follow the same path hers did and nor did I wish my kids to be a victim of any form of abuse. Although I knew that I had encountered many bad things in my life already, I wanted them to stop with me. I recognized that I was destined for greatness some time ago and I was determined to make the life of my children and generations to come better. It only takes God to use one person to cause a shift for an entire generation. Just as there are generational curses, there are generational blessings. It's my goal to leave a legacy for my children, grandchildren, great grandchildren and future generations of my family.

Buffering the Pain

Romans 8:18

For I reckon that the sufferings of this present time are not worthy to be compared with the glory which shall be revealed in us.

WE DON'T LIKE PAIN!!!!

There are some that can endure more pain than others, having a higher threshold of tolerance to pain, however I don't know of anyone that can honestly say, "I really enjoy being in pain". There are people that may self-inflict pain, such as cutters and those that attempt suicide, however, it is not because they enjoy pain but in fact the outer pain of the cutting gives them a release from the inner pain they are experiencing and those that attempt suicide are attempting to flee pain altogether. It is their only escape!

We as a people will use so many other methods to help us to escape pain. We use aspirin for relief from headaches, epidurals for relief from pain affiliated with childbirth, some use and abuse drugs and alcohol to escape pains of their past and life in general. We use drastic measures to flee pain. Human kind tends to shy from pain. In fact, we pray that God will shield us from pain, guard our hearts and deliver us from pain. Even Jesus prayed, anticipating the pain of His death on the cross, "Father if this cup pass me by…" but realizing it is all a part of the process He said "your will be done". We must too realize that we cannot buffer all pain, that pain in fact is a part of the process. Pain is an indication that you are still alive and gives God a way to manifest Himself in our lives as a healer of our hearts, minds and bodies and a lifter of our heads.

My Pain is My Purpose

1 Peter 4:12-13

Beloved, do not think it strange concerning the fiery trial which is to try you, as though some strange thing happened to you, but rejoice to the extent that you partake of Christ's suffering, that when his glory is revealed, you may also be glad with exceeding joy.

Life is Pain!!

Life, as long as we are living, can guarantee some level of pain. If we stump our toe, that is painful; a headache, especially a migraine, is painful all in the physical sense. We can also experience heart ache, which indeed is painful and in some instances more difficult to overcome. The list goes on and on regarding different pains we may experience on this journey through life.

Most are typically some form of pain we endure for a reason, but then there are times in life we endure great pain that has a purpose. For example, the pain of childbirth. Great pain but the purpose is to bring forth life, a child. The greatest example of pain with a purpose is the pain of the cross Jesus endured. He was beaten, spit on, well you know the story and the purpose of his pain was to fulfill the prophecy and to save all mankind. The thing about the pain Jesus endured was that it was in no way beneficial to him. Neither the pain nor the purpose was directly beneficial to him. He came to this world with the sole purpose of dying for the sins of the whole world so that we may live.

Many times in life we go through painful experiences and we often wonder why. We say, "Well God I'm saved, I pay my tithes, I love everyone as you've commanded, I feed the hungry….I'm not perfect but I'm saved so why am I enduring this much pain?" In some cases, we reflect back over our lives and say, "God, I was an innocent child, why would you have allowed such a thing to happen to me?" It is not until we get to the other side of pain that we realize it had a purpose. In many instances, like Jesus, we endure pain, which has nothing to do with us directly but is connected to our purpose and our ministries. The pain of lacking, always having a need, growing up poor can be a ministry attesting to the fact that God is a provider; going through life sick and being healed can lead to the attestation of God being a healer, etc.

We all have endured some pain in life. If you have not yet I have two words for you "keep living." We can either allow this pain to make us bitter or better. When we can acknowledge that pain has a purpose and continue to seek God through it all, then and only then can we allow ourselves to be healed by God and to testify of God's goodness. It gives us the testimony of how He is able to bring us to the other side of pain. We are able to share our stories and our glories.

God, the Fixer of everything broken

My journey through life has encountered many challenges, some seeming harder to overcome than others. Two of the most challenging for me were overcoming being the victim of sexual abuse and surviving domestic violence, both at the hands of men I loved and thought I could trust. As it regards the sexual abuse, this very person was found in a place where most people seek refuge; the place where you are supposed to find peace, the place where God is supposed to rest and abide…the Church! My abuse was administered by someone we thought was "called", "saved", "a man of God." He was a leader in the church I attended growing up. I spent much of my life and many days at church, more than the average child. This was due to my great-grandmother, the woman who raised me playing such an active role in the church and community. As she was about the church's business, this leader would lure me into his office and begin to do "his business." Later I realized that it was not only me, but several of my associates in encountering the very same thing. I discovered this from the associates that I stayed in touch with. God only knows who else may have fallen victim to this man!

I felt hopeless! Who would believe me if I said I was being touched and sexually abused by this leader, this pillar of the community. This man was well respected and loved at the church and in the community at large. The only people I was able to talk to were my church friends. Unfortunately, we were all going through the same thing which meant none of us could save the others; our level of pain was equivalent.

This lead me to find other methods of crying out, reaching out. I started to drown my pain in alcoholic beverages. At least after I drank I did not feel as much pain as I did when I was sober. At some point, my great-grandmother discovered the emptied alcohol bottles and knew that I had been drinking. When she discovered that I had been drinking, I thought she would certainly understand and somehow discover what I had been enduring. I hoped that she would see this as my cry for help and she would do just that, she would help me. Certainly, my grandmother knows me and would understand my unspoken words and translate my tearless cries, but she did not.

There was certainly a language barrier in place in which she translated my drinking to mean I was out of control and would soon be like my mother. Feeling as if she could not change the path of my life, she transferred custody of me over to my maternal grandmother. Upon moving in with my grandmother, my life experienced a major overhaul and not in a positive way. I was shifted from a predominately Caucasian school to a predominately African American school (can you say culture shock). My grandmother was a lot less nurturing than my great-grandmother; it was very different, not as pleasant but was very necessary.

The pain associated with being a victim of sexual abuse as a child set the pace for my life and made me stronger. The abuse, neglect, and trials all prepared me for who

I am today. The pain of all of my life's trials had a purpose that has allowed me to be compassionate towards abused youth.

My pain was not designed to kill me but to perfect me and build compassion for the suffering of others.

Today I act as an advocate and a voice for youth that have experienced abuse in any form (physically, sexually, and verbally) and for those that fall victim to human trafficking.

Each year, in the month of April, Center of Empowerment along with myself the Board Chair of COE observe Child Abuse Awareness Month, making others aware of what our children are encountering and encouraging others to use their voice and advocate for our children. Saving our futures, start with YOUth!!! It is my hope to save youth from encountering the abuse that I received as a child so that have a better chance to live more productive lives.

Although my pain was not meant to kill me it did not stop the enemy from trying…

Let me tell you a story of a young lady. She was preparing for her senior year in college. She met her prince charming at a vulnerable time in her life. During this time, she was in school full-time while caring for her great-grandmother whose health was deteriorating rapidly and caring for her five-year-old son. Her great-grandmother raised her from the age of two months old and was the one she called mother. She was also serving as the president of her sorority, a member of SGA, and an active member of number of other organizations.

As they tend to be, her prince charming was handsome, polite, and said all of the right things. He appeared to be to be a gentleman and a family man. He wined and dined her, showed interest in getting to know her child, but her son refused to get to know him. The first two months their relationship was awesome. He asked her to move in with him and she did because she was in love. She was so in love that she did not pay attention to how her son was feeling about the situation.

Two days after meeting her beau, she was asked to meet his family. Her prince came from an influential family in the community. Everything seemed so perfect. Out of the blue, a few days later his sister calls and warns the girl to be careful because her brother used to be volatile with his ex wife. The angry young lady confronted her beau who denied the claims and countered that his sister did not like him and that his mother was physically abusive which is why his sister was lying on him.

A few weeks later, they young woman noticed a change in his mannerisms. He began to tell her where she could and could not go and who she could talk to. He began showing up unannounced to her classes to see if she was there. He began questioning and interrogating her as to what time she would be home. When she told others about these behaviors, his personality was so smooth and charming that everyone around her felt she was exaggerating his actions except his family. He was very obsessive about his military career and pleasing his father. He stated that he had a love hate relationship with his mother because she use to beat him on his hands with spoons.

One evening while they were driving to the local mall, they passed one of her fraternity brothers in his car. As the cars passed each other, her frat brother blew his horn at her as a polite gesture of speaking. Her prince commanded her to turn around and go home. Upon entering the apartment, he punched a hole in the wall and pushed her in the bedroom. He choked and raped her all the time of accusing her of cheating on him. Once he calmed down, he blamed her for his actions and reactions.

Shortly thereafter, her great-grandmother was placed into ICU. The prince wanted her to choose between her great-grandmother and him. She, of course, chose to go see her and received a beating on her return home for that. Her great-grandmother passed away the next day. Her family called for her to come to the hospital. Still, her beau was reluctant to bring her. Nevertheless, she made it to her family and they laid the mantle on her to make the arrangements for the funeral out of town where her great-grandmother lived. She was going to be gone for a week. While she was out of town, she attempted to reach the prince but their conversations were limited. He refused to support her and attend the funeral. He blamed her for leaving him behind, not being home to cook for him, and making sure that he was taken care of. When she returned home, she received another beating.

As a matter of fact, from that day on, she was beaten at least four times a week just because. Sometimes she was beaten in front of her son and sometimes not. He loved to choke her, telling her, "It gave him a rush." During this period, the young lady had very limited contact with her family and friends. She could only go to school and work. She could not attend any functions without him. In front of her family and friends, he would act like he loved her so much. But when they were alone, his dark side and anger would come out. During the duration of the relationship, she began to notice her son's behavior decline as he appeared to be becoming angry and violent.

In her spring semester of college, the young woman's professors decided to confront her about the decline that they were observing in her work. Her grades were failing and her smile was no longer there. She was skipping class and not turning in assignments. Her family valued education highly, so when she received her failing progress report and seeing the fear on her son's face, she decided to leave the prince. She told him she was leaving to which he responded it was fine, "Go". As she turned and walked away, she was caught by shock and surprise as he suddenly appeared, placing a butcher knife to her throat. This would be the day she found out with all certainty that God had her back. She prayed to God that if HE got her out of that situation she would not ever return. She held her ground and calmly reminded him that she worked for law enforcement and in the judicial system. She reminded him that if he killed her, it would not go unnoticed, that federal, state, and local law enforcement would be looking for him all over the place. He dropped the knife and left the apartment. The young lady called her mom and explained the horror that she had been living. Her mother advised her that if she was in her shoes that she would leave.

She stated that it was her choice and that she would back her. That day was the day that she left and moved back home.

She filed criminal charges against him along with a restraining order. He was arrested and he tried to get her family especially, her grandparents to convince her to drop the charges. Her grandmother took his side and stated that he was too nice to have done all of those things.

Despite all of the pressure, she refused to drop the charges and her relationship with her family, especially her grandmother was strained (including no contact) for two years. His family was upset that she pressed charges as well. After going back and forth on the court case for six months, she decided to drop the case and move away for a fresh start.

In this story, our "Prince Charming" turned out to be real toad! And as you might have guessed already my dear reader, the young lady in this story, was me!!

In the name of Love…

Things we allow ourselves to endure, in the name of love. Abuse for me did not stop at the sexual abuse I experienced as a child. I also endured physical abuse at the hands of someone who I loved with all my heart and I thought loved me. This man was a breath of fresh air and the answer to my prayers, so I thought. He ended up being what the Bible describes as a wolf in sheep's clothing.

I dated this guy for a while and realized he is "the one." After dating for some time, he proposed that we should move in together and I decided it was time to meet the families. I met his and he met mine. As I stated earlier, upon meeting my family, my grandmother warned me that I had better know what I was doing and his sister warned me to run. Well that did not go as I anticipated, however I was in love and we moved forward with our lives together. After living together for some time, I began to see the signs and understood the warnings, he was an abuser. He would verbally, mentally and physically abuse me for any reason he thought was appropriate, yet I stayed with him because I loved him and bought into the, "I won't do it again" ritual of lies. The longer I stayed, the more intense and the more frequent the beatings were and ultimately he pulled a knife on me and threatened to kill me!

After a period of suffering physically and academically because my grades had began to decline in college, I decided it was time to get out. I initially turned to my family, who did not believe me and thought it was impossible for such a good guy to be doing what I said he was doing.

This added to the pain I was already suffering. I then turned to the courts for help; however trial after trial were continuously delayed. I figured it was because he came from a prestigious well-known family. Betrayed by my family, the justice system and ultimately by the man I love, I had nowhere else to turn, so I left! Packed up and moved to Texas for a new start, a new beginning, to turn a new leaf in life.

This story wraps up for me about two years later, when I received a call from my grandmother apologizing for not believing in me. She stated that the feds were looking for me after reviewing my case against my ex. They wanted to notify me that they had arrested him for a murder that he had committed in a domestic violence case before dating me. They stated that he has a history of domestic violence and violence towards women. At that moment, I felt a release. The chain of fear had finally been broken.

Although I changed my environment, I did not realize I was still bringing the same old me which meant my results would still be the same. The Bible speaks of the renewing of your mind and how it causes true change to manifest. I missed the importance of that particular scripture. While in Texas, I met a Preacher, he was a true gentleman and again the answer to another prayer. He would help me to escape my past and overcome the trauma I endured at the hand of the last man I had been in a relationship with. I would be "The Preacher's Wife."

The Purpose

As you were able to see, I have endured much pain in my life, much at the hands of "man" and indeed, I could have given in to the pain and been bitter all my days. However, I read in Romans 8:28 which says "And we know that all things work together for good for those that love God, for those that are the called according to his purpose". This verse indicates to me that everything in my life, though it may not be good that it will in some way work out for my good. In some way the good and the bad will join together and do me a favor. Somehow God will make the negative and the positive join forces and the positive will cancel out the negative. (Ain't God alright??) This has helped me to see my pain was not designed to kill me nor oppress nor depress me, but it had and still has a purpose.

Focus On Solutions, Not Problems

One of the things I did during my most painful days was spending a lot of time thinking about my problems. I turned them over in my head again and again, focusing on what was wrong. It's very easy to fall into this trap, where all you do is worry about your problems and feel sorry for yourself -- I know I was guilty of that. Indeed, it is human nature, but it is also not very helpful. Imagine if I would have stayed a prisoner to that mindset. I would still be crying today about how unfair life is never moving into purpose, constantly living in the pain.

There is no point in obsessing about your problems. All that energy and brainpower should be focused on a solution! When my life was falling apart around me, I sought refuge. This time I did not seek refuge in alcoholic beverages, I sought Christ, my savior, deliverer, and ever present help in the time of trouble.

After all I had been through, I was able to take a self-assessment and see that my good days outweighed my bad. This helped me to change the way I looked at my life. I went from thinking in terms of the good and bad to ways of resolving the issues in my life then on to how can I use my problems to help others. I began to see that this thing was bigger than me. When I began to seek God and ask how can I help someone else, I no longer felt the pain associated with my experiences! The pain had now been converted to fuel for my purpose!

This is something you can do in order to get to the other side of your pain! It is quite possible that you are alone and that you did not go through this for you! God is not vindictive to make you go through a trial just because. He trusts that you will allow Him to heal you and that you will use your testimony to heal others. Try this when something in your life seems overwhelming, take a self-assessment. Sit down with paper and pen and write the vision, make it plain as the Bible says. Make a list of what has happened in your life and next to the problems begin to create solutions and how you can use it to help yourself and others.

Make Your Life About the Future, Not the Past

It is very hard to let go of your past, but know this "as long as you live there you cannot get to the future God has promised you!" The past has passed and should not be your prison. We too often become prisoners of our past pain and past experiences. This hinders our ability to move forward in life. That does not mean forget your past experiences or the lessons because that is impossible. It means press forward without continuing to look back. Letting go of your past is a long, hard process and something you must continue to do daily. I'm still a work in progress in that area.

Moving on from the pain and troubles of your past takes a lot of time. The past is not something you can stick in a microwave and zap in a minute or two. It takes a lot of effort to put your past where it needs to be -- behind you. Nevertheless, here is why it is important that we put the past behind us, because if we live in the past, we will never discover or reach our destiny.

Destiny, promise, potential, purpose -- all of these are things that have to do with the future, not the past. If we continue to dwell in our past, because we are not omniscient, we cannot live in two places at one time, therefore we will never enjoy the gift of the present and definitely not the future.

"Humble yourselves, therefore, under the mighty hand of God," it says in 1 Peter 5:6-7, "so that at the proper time He may exalt you, casting all your anxieties on Him, because He cares for you."

We need to surrender our anxieties, our problems and our past to God -- so that He can exalt us and raise us to a new and better place. Only by living our lives based on the future, and not on the past, can we allow this exaltation to happen.

So work on changing the way you think about what matters in life: Not everything that came before, but everything that is still to come in God's glory!

Plan of the Enemy

Luke 22:31-32

And the Lord said, Simon, Simon, behold, Satan hath desired to have you, that he may sift you as wheat. But I have prayed for thee, that thy faith fail not: and when thou art converted, strengthen thy brethren.

Plan A and Plan B

There are two plans revolving around your life, one from your creator and one from your enemy. God's plan for you was formed before the creation of the world. His plan is everlasting, unchanging, and includes all things. God's plan included His judgment, His condemnation, His deliverance, His redemption, and His forgiveness.

Satan has a plan for you as well. Satan, since his fall, has tried to create separation and distance between you and God. Satan has placed himself strongly as an adversary against mankind. Satan tried to short circuit God's plan of salvation by tempting our Savior. Satan works to keep you bound, lost, unseeing and unknowing of the chains he has slowly, gently wrapped around you to firmly in the place he wants you.

Satan knows however, that he has no authority; he can do nothing without God's permission. So ultimately, even Satan's broad machinations, become a part of God's larger plan, to draw you closer to Him, and closer to your destiny.

John 8:44 tells us "he's a murderer from the beginning and does not stand in the truth, because there is not truth in him. Whenever he speaks a lie, he speaks from his own nature, for he is a liar and the father of lies".

II Corinthians 11:3 tells us that but "I am afraid that, as the serpent deceived Eve by his craftiness, our minds will be led astray from the simplicity and purity of devotion to Christ".

The devil does his work by attacking the mind. If he can kill our will through our thoughts then we are no longer effective. This is why God tells us that if we can keep our minds stayed on him, he will keep us in perfect peace. God also tells us that we can be changed by the renewing of our minds. Satan is fully aware of what the word says and God's purpose for our lives. He knows Proverbs 23:7 says "for as a man thinks within himself, so he is".

To steal......

At the age of sweet 16, we are beginning to enjoy life, some freedoms from parents; many begin to explore different relationships and much more. It was no different for my mom except the fact that she had made a grown up decision to engage in sex as a result and became a mother.

Well as you know, the old folks in that time had their own sets of beliefs and my great-grand and grandmother were no different. My great grandmother did not believe a girl should be raised in the home with a male that was not her father, which meant she was unhappy with my mother's choice to date someone else other than my father. My mother not only dated another man but she decided to live with him which was a definite no-no for my great-grandmother therefore she took me from my mother. At the time I was only 6 months old, so I did not have a say in the matter. Her rationale for doing so was to save me from making the same mistakes that my mother had and she opted to raise me.

In her quest to assure that I was nothing like my mother, my great-grandmother offered me an abundance of things. She enrolled me in the best of schools, predominantly white private schools and provided many things. To assure that I did not feel lack, my Grandfather & Uncles would come to get me to provide a positive male influence in my life.

As you can see, I had more than the average child. I was afforded many opportunities, yet for me that still did not help me. What I struggled with had nothing to do with lack yet it was an internal struggle.

There were things that my great-grandmother tried her best to protect me from. However there were unseen dangers that lurked in the very place I thought was a safe haven. The place where you think all good people go, yet in this place I was being robbed of my innocence. The place where God lives known as the church.

To kill…

Had the devil had any control in the matter, he would have killed me. He actually could have used me to kill me. I could have done so with alcoholic beverages because I started drinking at an early age. It could have been through many avenues however, God would not allow it to be so. God interjected on my behalf a long time ago and though he allowed me to endure a lot, the trials came to make me strong; they were not designed to kill me.

The devil is fully aware that he cannot kill us physically because the blood of Jesus covers us. Therefore what he does is kill all that we stand for and who we are. There are several target areas in our lives determined to rob us of. If he manages to hurt us and take from us it will ultimately result in our demise. One area is, **Purpose** because our purpose is our mere reason. Another is for existing, which is, we are worthless without it. **Vision** is what is used to give us fuel, hope and propel us to our destination, purpose. Lack of vision causes complacency and lack of thriving. **Your children** are a vulnerable spot because if the devil can attack your children you cannot focus on your vision or purpose. It's the distraction needed to keep you out of focus and away from your place of purpose. **Faith** is a target area because without faith it's not only impossible to please God but without it you lose the ability to expect the great from God. If you expect nothing, you then ask for nothing and end up getting nothing. The Bible teaches that if we ask we shall receive which is the last thing the enemy wants you to do. **Your voice** the devil is aware that God has given us the power to speak to our situations, the ability to speak life and that life and death is in the power of our tongues. Therefore if we can speak it and believe then we'll have whatever we desire. If the devil can silence us and take our voices, then he has taken our power to speak things into existence and to speak life. That which is without life is ultimately dead. This is the desired end for us the devil desires.

Finally, the enemy wants **Your Destiny**. Many times the devil knows your fate before you do. He knows your destiny and will do all he can to keep you from getting to it. He uses attacks, distractions and many other tactics, but if we are able to keep our minds on God and trust in God to do all that He said He will do in our lives we can reach our destinies. It is totally purposeless for us to die with our destinies when there are so many people here on earth that can benefit from it. We therefore have to learn to rebuke Satan consistently, start recognizing his attacks and give the problems to God and leave them there. Our futures, destinies and good living are there for the taking, the question is who is going to take them, you or the enemy?

To destroy….

You remember the story of my prince charming. That took place during my senior year of college. As I said earlier, he was nice looking and very charming and the answer to my prayers. He came at a time when my life was sort of stressful because I was in the cycle of caring for my son and attending school. I was also caring for my great-grandmother who raised me but now she needed me because she had fallen and broken her hip. The responsibilities were a lot, so this man was a breath of fresh air, my prince charming. My prince came to rescue me from the chaos of life that at the time would come to know. I was in love.

As the story went, after three months, it was time to meet the families; I met his family and he met mine. Upon meeting his family, they were prestigious and warm however, remember that from somewhere out of left field one of his sisters warned me "you better run." I was thinking, "Wow I did not expect that" but seeing him as the great person I had come to know, I brushed it off. When I mentioned it to him later, he said she was the sister he did not get along with—the epitome of sibling rivalry is what I attributed it to.

Well now, it is time for him to meet my great-grandmother because he has now asked that I move in with him. Great-grandmother also warns, "You'd better know what you are doing." Another warning that I shrug off, attributing her warning to that of a caring yet overly concerned grandmother.

We moved forward and I move in with my prince, life is great up until the representative moved out and the real person moved in. He was just the monster sister and great-grandmother warned me about. He began to become physically and verbally abusive from August to March I endured severe abuse at the hands of the man I once thought was an answer to my prayers. I had no one to educate me on how to deal with domestic violence so I stayed in that situation way too long. I stayed long enough for my grades to decline, for me to threaten failure in college, for me to become a victim of domestic violence. This relationship was terminated quickly when my ex-boyfriend placed a knife at my throat. I had no one to educate me on how to deal with domestic violence. The only thing I knew was the legal side of putting him jail.

The devil will not only try to destroy you physically but he will attempt to destroy your will. If he can lie to you enough and you begin to believe that you are incapable of succeeding or incapable of doing all things as Christ has stated, then he has won.

The Master's Plan

Jeremiah 1:5

I knew you before I formed you in your mother's womb. Before you were born, I set you apart and appointed you as my prophet to the nations.

The Best Laid Plans...

We go through life and we make plans. We plan to finish school; we plan our careers, weddings, family functions, Plan, Plan, Plan. Many times, we even "think" we plan out our entire lives and every intricate component of it. I am sure this is extremely tickling to God. He admires our initiative and tenacity; however, he doesn't need our help. I once heard an old Pastor say, "if you want to make God laugh, show him your plans".

We hear things like if you fail to plan, plan to fail which is really a good philosophy. It's good because we cannot go through life just winging it. We need some type of structure and a blue print in life to work from, but not before consulting God to determine what is it that he will have you to do. It is quite often that our plans for our lives do not coincide with what God has planned for us. Ephesians 2:10 tells us *"We are His workmanship, created in Christ Jesus for good works, which God prepared beforehand, that we should walk in them."* This affirms that we were created to do well, but we must seek him to determine what the good work actually is.

Too often, we follow our own agendas, which causes us to simply spin our wheels and waste precious time because we are doing what we think is our purpose yet we are operating outside of the will of God for our lives. I did say "we" because I am just as guilty and after talking with many people, I know that I am not alone. This is because we did not "seek" prior to "doing". The order is seek and do however, we do and then seek when we have run into a brick wall. Thank God for mercies that endure; that he still answers even when we call him and seek from the brick walls we have caused ourselves to make a head on collision with.

God has several plans for us and his will is always in our best interest. One of his desires is that we not get drunk with wine, for that is debauchery, but be filled with the Spirit (Ephesians 5:16-18). Knowing God's will definitely involves us knowing that God wants us to be holy.

Secondly, if you are a believer you also understand that it is the will of God, according to Ephesians 5, that you live clean and filled with the Holy Spirit. Knowing God's will means that we are walking in holiness.

Romans 12:1-2 - "Therefore, I urge you, brothers, in view of God's mercy, to offer your bodies as living sacrifices, holy and pleasing to God - this is your spiritual act of worship. Do not conform any longer to the pattern of this world, but be transformed by the renewing of your mind. Then you will be able to test and approve what God's will is - **his good, pleasing and perfect will.**" According to this verse, knowing God's will involves knowing that his good and perfect will comes by us being transformed by the renewing of our minds.

His word says that he stands at the door (of our hearts) and knocks hoping that we will answer. He desires that we seek him first and that we put him first in everything we do. If we put him first in all that we do, then he will add all things needed unto us. God also states that above all things he desires for us to prosper and to be in good health. God is our father and he desires nothing the best for his children.

..Plans to prosper you and not to harm you

My journey from trial to triumph has been challenging and at points rather difficult. In spite of the difficulties, in every lesson there has been a blessing. In maturing and learning more about God, I understand that he allows his children to endure challenges that are not designed to destroy us as the devil will have us to believe, but to strengthen you. In his word, he tells us the afflictions of the righteous are many, but that he would deliver us from them all.

God also assures us that all things work together for good for those that love God and are called according to his purpose. This gives us an assurance in knowing that even the bad things we endure, in the end will combine with all the good and work in our favor. I have had many good and bad situations that I have endured growing up and did not understand this philosophy in my years of youth.

When we were in school, in math class we were taught about integers. The process taught that multiplying two positive numbers would give you a positive answer. Even multiplying two negative numbers would give you a positive. Yet when you multiply a negative number to a positive number, you would end up with a negative number. That simply put tells us that the negative would cancel out the positive.

We can very well parallel this very same philosophy to life in general because many of us believe that when bad things happen in life, it is all doom and gloom and see no hope. I admit that when I have encountered trials in my life, it did not seem as if it was working for me. Actually, I prayed much of it away from me, only desiring the good. I prayed for the blessings and promises of God not realizing the bad just as much as the good was all a part of the process that would form me and make me who I am today.

Oh no…this positive is negative

I took the test and it gave a positive result. Test taken by the doctor, and again results were positive but these positive results were crushing to me. I was seventeen years old, beginning to live my life and a Senior in high school. I had been waiting for this time in my life to enjoy my last year in high school, senior prom, class trip you know all the fun festivities we enjoy in senior year, so this positive was not good.

This was not a positive score on my ACT to get into college. Neither was it a positive score on a test in class, assuring I would graduate on time. This positive was indeed a negative, a double negative. It was a pregnancy test with a positive result but how, I had only "done it" one time how did this happen? Yes, I was pregnant.

I was a senior, single, seventeen and PREGNANT! Instead of being crowned Prom Queen, I was received the title of "Mother" in my senior year of high school. I had become a mother prior to completing my Senior year at the age 17 which means I had already began my journey into motherhood and followed the pattern of my mother. This is the pattern that my great grandmother and grandmother tried so hard to prevent me from falling into. I was now a single mother prior to finishing my childhood and prior to completing high school.

They say……

According to statistics, my future was bleak. Actually according to the statistics, I was already destined for failure from the time I was born. They say "teenage mothers are less likely to complete high school and are more likely to end up on welfare (nearly 80 percent of unmarried teen mothers end up on welfare). Also, the children of teen parents are more likely to perform poorly in school and are at greater risk of abuse and neglect. The sons of teen mothers are 13 percent more likely to end up in prison while teen daughters are 22 percent more likely to become teen mothers themselves".

Well, according to what they said, since I was the daughter of a teen mother it meant I was 22 percent more likely to become a teen mother and I did. I repeated the cycle and that is where I decided to get off the spinning wheel and break the cycle. In spite of what "they" said, I knew God said something different and had a different path for my life. I knew that I was destined for greatness and that above all things God wished that I would prosper and not to fail as "they" said.

But God says…

I had to choose whose report I was going to believe, that of man which stated I was doomed to fail or God who told me I can do all things through him because he would strengthen me to do so.

John 14:12-14
"Verily, verily, I say unto you, **He that believeth on me, the works that I do shall he do also; and greater works than these shall he do;** *because I go unto my Father. And whatsoever ye shall ask in my name, that will I do, that the Father may be glorified in the Son. If ye shall ask any thing in my name, I will do it."* This scripture revealed to me that all I had to do was ask for a better life, to live a life of purpose and that it would be given to me.

I thank God that my story was not written by man and has played out far different from what the statistics show. I am indeed the product of teen parents and I became a teen mother. That component of what statistics reported does hold some truth but that is where the truth started and ended for me. Fortunately for me, I was reared initially by my great-grandparents and later by grandparents that were much more mature and spiritually grounded. Though my life still took the same route to teen parenting, I was still spiritually grounded.

My parents later established other relationships separate from one another but my mother and step-father remained an active force and support system in my life. I had a strong support system with two sets of grandparents, several uncles, my mother and step-father. The adults in my life assured that I received a sound education and an established relationship with and understanding of God.

Attending church in my family was not an option but a mandate. I was born into a family of Pastors and active Church leaders, which meant I grew up in ministry and was always actively involved in some way. I have had the privilege of serving as an International Youth Pastor, Women Ministry Leader and Praise Team Leader. I attribute my life's journey and the accomplishments thereof to the support of the family God blessed me with and ultimately to God and the favor that He has shown me.

Being a mother poses its own set of complexities, but being a single teenage mother causes those challenges to multiply. Had it not been for the support of my family, I could have succumbed to the statistics that state that I would have had to drop out of school to care for my son and follow the same negative sequence of events defined by those that created the statistics. I am eternally grateful for the support and love of my family and the favor of God, which has allowed me to overcome many challenges that would have consumed most. My family not only provided me the support I needed to complete school but also taught me the necessary parenting skills I so desperately needed. I am proud to say that I completed high school with honors and went on to further my education, something that "they" say does not happen for teen mothers.

The fact that I completed high school on time is significant because it demonstrates

I was able to defeat the odds. Statistics or should I say "they" say, teen mothers don't finish school and ultimately fail academically, however I finished High school and beyond. I initially earned a Bachelor of Science degree in Psychology and Criminal Justice. I later pursued and earned an Executive M.B.A. in Healthcare Management, Clinical Masters' Degree in Social Work with a specialization in Disaster Mental Health, Master Certification in Forensic Psychology, Nonprofit Management, a Doctorate in Divinity as well as countless certifications. The road God has ordained for me has not been traveled with ease, however with God, family, self-determination, motivation and the desire to succeed, I've been able to accomplish that which others have said could not be done. So tell me, "Whose report will you believe?" Man says, "You cannot", but God says, "We can" do all things through Christ because he strengthens us to do so. Since we know the devil is a liar and incapable of telling the truth, anything that does not line up with God's word of us being capable of doing all things or his declaration of prosperity for our lives, WE SHOULD NOT BELIEVE!!!!!

Plans to give you hope and a future

From my teen-age encounters, it seemed as if the odds were not in my favor. In all actuality, the odds were stacked against me. However, at this point in my life, as I reflect and look back, I see I not only overcame but by the grace of God, I defeated the odds. The sequence of events in my life not only helped me to defeat the odds but it left a legacy for my children and generations to come that I pray will follow in my footsteps.

Though my oldest was the product of a single teen mother, he too has defeated the odds. He has graduated high school at the age of 16, is an entrepreneur with his own entertainment company and is presently in pursuit of his first college degree. My other children are still in school and all are positively engaged in different activities ever in pursuit of success. I must say that my hard work and many sacrifices has and is still paying off. They have not only paid off for the sake of me and my family but for all the youth and families I have had the privilege of servicing. My calling is not to arrive at a destination of stability, but to travel a pathway of constant growth and transformation. God has merely used me as a vessel and my life as a demonstration of what He is capable of doing and who He is. None of what I have accomplished has been on my own, it is all GOD!!

Therefore, I want to encourage you that when things in your life become difficult, look at it as an opportunity to grow, transition and become stronger and wiser. The Bible teaches that trials come to make us strong, they build character. I excite, motivate and encourage those entrusted in my care to live a fulfilled life! I continue to display a passion and fire for advocating on the behalf of victims of Child Abuse and Domestic Violence especially for teens, college students, young mothers and women who have survived D.V. This is truly one of my passions because as my story shows, I too am a survivor of D.V. Yes, I am a survivor of Domestic Violence!

I am very transparent which makes me very effective in what I do. I am the President of RARE, Inc., an organization committed to the personal development of young women, in which I have served as mentor for young women who have experienced trauma through sexual assault and/or domestic violence. I am dedicated to training young women by using practical and biblical principles, empowering them to live a fulfilled and enriched life. My God given talents and gifts are to empower lives and heal hearts!

I have worked in the children services' field for at least 12 years. I serve as the Board Chair for Center of Empowerment for Families & Youth, Inc. COE is a 501(C)(3) nonprofit organization that is dedicated to providing cultural enrichment, educational, counseling services, and case management services to low income and at risk families. One area we specialize in is serving children who have experienced abuse and/or neglect. We also work with families who are considered at risk. We are working towards improving the lives of children and families within our community. Please visit our website at www.coe4youth.org

and follow us on twitter at https://twitter.com/CenterofEmpower and on Facebook at http://www.facebook.com/centerof.empowerment.

In March 2012, I became a partner of PullCorp Media & Business Consulting Group. PullCorp is a client management and business consulting firm that maintains practice areas in consumer marketing, corporate communications, fashion, digital/social media, crisis PR and entertainment. PullCorp's clients consist of models, music artists, motivational speakers, fitness trainers, & businesses to name a few. There is a new division coming in 2013. We are "Reaching beyond the limits of success" for our clients! Please follow us facebook at http://www.facebook.com/pull.corp &

twitter at https://twitter.com/PullCorpMedia.

Though I was a teen mother, today I am Dr. T. Pullum affectionately known as "Dr. CSI" or "Boss Lady" depending on the business setting. I am a Certified Child Abuse Forensic Investigator and a Certified Family Conflict Resolution Mediator. I hold various credentials and certifications. I work alongside Law Enforcement & social service agencies assisting victims of child abuse & Domestic Violence. I serve on several boards and advisory committees. I have a book that I coauthored entitled "It Takes a Village to Raise a Child: An Afrocentric Approach". To honor my work in the community, I recently received a Proclamation from the House of Representatives & the Mayor's Office. I am a Wife, Mother, Servant, Life Coach, Mentor, Entertainment Entrepreneur, and Business Consultant & Advocate. These are just a few of the titles that are used to characterize myself. You now know some of the story and the glory of Dr. C. Pullum.

I published this book, Breaking the Chains: From Hurting to Healing to show that even those that have "arrived" in life have encountered some struggles, difficulties and overcome some hurdles to accomplish their levels of success. Pain can be fuel for your life's purpose if you allow it to!! Push pass your pain and live, love and laugh!! You owe to yourself to LIVE!!! I have shared my accomplishments so that you can see how good God actually is. I want you to know that God can turn your pain into purpose and that your story can be used for his glory. Continue reading as the story of my life unfolds. I pray that it blesses your life!!

The Chains are Broken

1 Peter 5:10

May the God of all grace, who called us to His eternal glory by Christ Jesus, after you have suffered a while, perfect, establish, strengthen and settle you.

Whom the Son Sets Free….

In my distress I called on the Lord; the Lord answered me and set me free.

Galatians 5:13 For you were called to freedom, brothers. Only do not use your freedom as an opportunity for the flesh, but through love serve one another.

Romans 6:18 And, having been set free from sin, have become slaves of righteousness.

John 8:31-36 So Jesus said to the Jews who had believed in him, "If you abide in my word, you are truly my disciples, and you will know the truth, and the truth will set you free." They answered him, "We are offspring of Abraham and have never been enslaved to anyone. How is it that you say, 'You will become free'?" Jesus answered them, "Truly, truly, I say to you, everyone who commits sin is a slave to sin. The slave does not remain in the house forever; the son remains forever.

Ephesians 2:8-9 For by grace you have been saved through faith. And this is not your own doing; it is the gift of God, not a result of works, so that no one may boast.

Romans 6:7 For one who has died has been set free from sin.

Acts 13:38-39 Let it be known to you therefore, brothers, that through this man forgiveness of sins is proclaimed to you, and by him everyone who believes is freed from everything from which you could not be freed by the law of Moses.

2 Corinthians 3: 17 Now the Lord is the Spirit, and where the Spirit of the Lord is, there is freedom

And lastly…….

Galatians 5:1 It is for freedom that Christ has set us free. Stand firm, then, and do not let yourselves be burdened again by a yoke of slavery.

In Isaiah 40:5 the Bible speaks of the glory of the Lord being revealed, but this is only after the crooked places being made straight and the rough places, plain. This is an indication that we will have to endure some tough, hurting, difficult and painful times in life before we get to God's promised place for us.

The children of Israel went through the process for 40 years, the woman with the issue of blood 12 long years and the disciples went through the storm to get to the promise of getting to the other side. We must believe in God's word that says he will never leave nor forsake us and the fact that he's a God that cannot lie. That if he gives us a promise, no matter how hurtful or painful the process is the prophecy for our lives has to be fulfilled.

So many of us are still battling with chains, not physical but mental and emotional chains. Chains of oppression from our past, past abuse, neglect, generational curses, abandonment, bad relationships, miserable jobs, missed opportunities and other bad experiences that we allow to hold us hostage.

We tend to blame ourselves for bad experiences, see ourselves as not worthy of our callings or the good God has promised us. Many of our chains were inherited due to our upbringings, challenges and limitations imposed upon us when we were children. We become mentally handicapped by the "no you cannot do this" or "if I were you I would not do that" and we tend to drag our past baggage into our present and futures.

At some point, the family and past are no longer the blame for the chains that keep us bound. As an adult, we begin to accept the roles we play in our lives and destinies. We must renew our minds in order to escape the grips of the chains that had us bound.

After several years, I have finally been able to be freed of the conditioned chains that that held me in servitude and abuse for so long; I have been freed of the chains that imprisoned and traumatized me with relief and gratitude for my freedom.

My journey may have some wondering why I did not escape sooner because I was not physically bound or locked. I had options available to me to escape the abusive relationship. I had an extremely supportive family, why did not I tell someone about the abusive church leader?? The answer is simple; I was conditioned to believe that was what my life was supposed to be.

As appalling as this story is, I feel that it reflects similarities in how most of us live. We are all conditioned in some way, shape or form. We all possess the invisible chains that hold us captive. Conditioning, what we believe to be true, it forms the very fabric of our being, how we process the information we receive and the behaviors we observe, will determine what our choice limitations will be.

Are any of us really truly free?? If there were no limits, no boundaries, no conditions or long held limiting beliefs. What would our lives be like?

Ponder that for a moment…

So…why are not you living like that today?

Who or what holds you hostage?

What chains are keeping you where you are?

When deep within, there is more to your life, that you are not living to your full potential. You are not in your place of purpose. Conditioning hinders our ability to fully create the life we truly want to be living, hinders our ability to be our true authentic selves, to be truly be free…

For me, I am held hostage by my limiting beliefs, my habitual patterns, my ego mind and fears all of which is conditioning an outdated, untruthful, trained way of thinking

No matter how often I say, "That's behind me now" or "I'll never slip back to that thought/habit/reaction because I know I can choose differently and think differently." It was not until I moved in a new direction or until I chose to be and live free that, I was truly able to experience freedom from the chains. I chose to be free.

We remain stuck, uncertain, unsure, and afraid of change, of pushing past all we know, to see and to grasp all that is available to us, all that we possess within.

It seems safer within the confines of our captivity at times or as we refer to it as our comfort zone. Yet if we are honest with ourselves, it is not that comfortable at all. Dangerously safe, complacent but trapped in our habits and our way of thinking. Victims of ourselves. Yet there are no visible chains, no locked doors, and no shackles.

You can live free!

Our inner work may help us to no longer believe this inner voice of unreason which will cause those conditioned beliefs to diffuse and our new actions will begin to shape our new, chain free lives. We can live completely free, as soon as we realize that Fear is actually False Expectations Appearing Real and that what we fear is not a reality, just what we create in our own minds.

My encounter with the chains was a battle on the forefront of my mind that held me hostage for so long, at some point, it felt never ending! Every day, I pray for God's continued blessings in my life and for the ability to live in limitless potential. This is the place my spirit is aware we are supposed to be, however, my flesh attempts to limit and confine me, prohibiting me from reaching my intended destiny.

My daily prayers and talks with God unlock the chains that continue to attempt to wrap themselves around me. Now that I realize the power of prayer and have an unshakeable relationship with God, these chains do not stand a chance. Through it all, I had God's promise to hold onto to get me from pain to this place called purpose. In the words of the gospel hymn, Praise the Lord, Hallelujah I'm free!!

About the Author

Wife; Mother; Servant; Vision Coach; Educator; Mentor; Advocate; and Film & Theatrical Producer. While any of these titles could describe Dr. Trina Pullum, when it comes to her life story, there's one word that stands out above them all: **Survivor**.

Dr. Pullum has been called a Trailblazer, Transformer, and a Visionary. Her life's mission to help women heal and grow their greatness! Dr. Pullum has an enlivening presence that compels people to stop allowing limits placed on them to hinder their growth toward becoming all that God destined them to be. Dr. Pullum uses her broad experience and successful track record to assist her clients in their needs.

Dr. Pullum is one of the powerful voices that God is raising up to empower others to discover what God has in store for them. As a visionary coach, executive mentor, trainer and empowered speaker, Dr. Pullum's thought provoking workshops are ones that will push you into your next level. Having overcome many challenges and trials that would have taken most out, Dr. Pullum displays a passion and fire for God that says God is absolutely in control. Through her testimony and life-changing messages delivered with passion, dignity and strength, in her own personal style will encourage and inspire you.

Dr. Pullum serves as one of the Executive Officers of PullCorp Media & Business Consulting Group where she specializes in artist management, music production, public relations, and business consulting.

She serves as the board chair of Center of Empowerment for Families & Youth, Inc., a non-profit dedicated to helping low-income and at-risk families. Dr. Pullum is also the founder of RARE Inc., an organization dedicated to empowering young women through training and personal development, using practical and biblical principles.

Dr. Pullum serves as the CEO of Puissance Maison Productions. Puissance Maison Productions is a company that offers film and video production services. Dr. Pullum has produced & directed several commercials, movies, and plays. She serves as a International Officer for the Full Gospel Baptist Fellowship. Dr. Pullum is affiliated with several organizations.

A New Orleans native and Tulane University Alumni, Dr. Pullum has been recognized for her life's work with proclamations from the House of Representatives and Office of Mayor-President and by other entities. Dr. Pullum's heart is to empower lives, heal the broken, and win souls for the Kingdom!

Please visit www.drcatrinapullum.com

For Dr. Pullum or a Breaking The Chains Media Kit, please email media@drcatrinapullum.com

For booking, please contact PullCorp Media Group at 225-366-7855

Made in the USA
San Bernardino, CA
14 January 2017